# Climbi

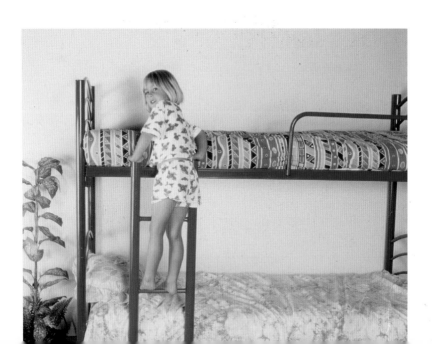

She is up
on the gate.

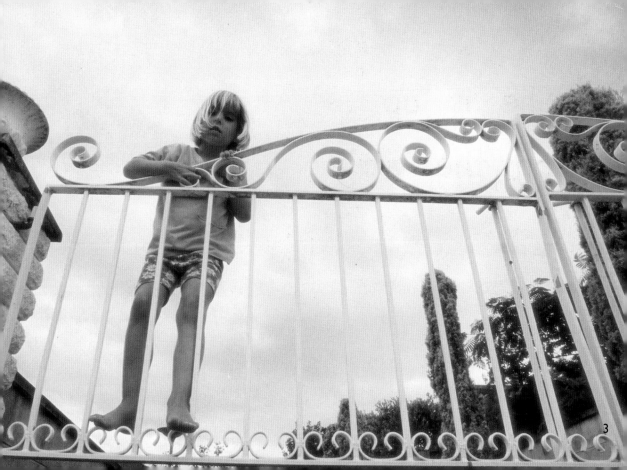

She is up
on the wall.

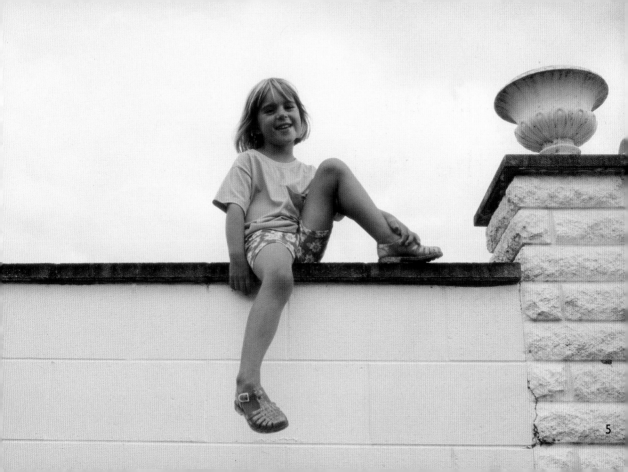

She is up
on the fort.

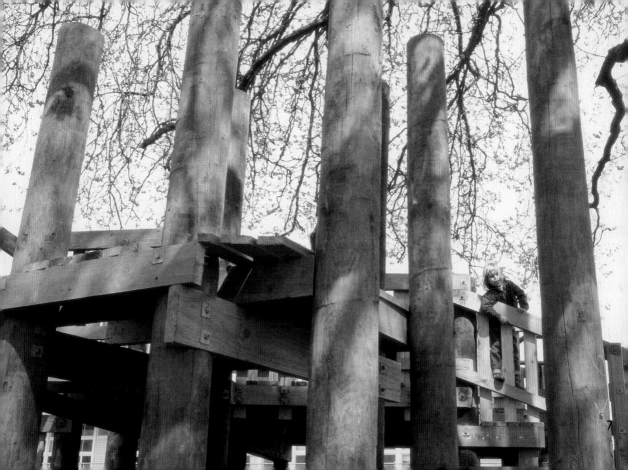

She is up

on the slide.

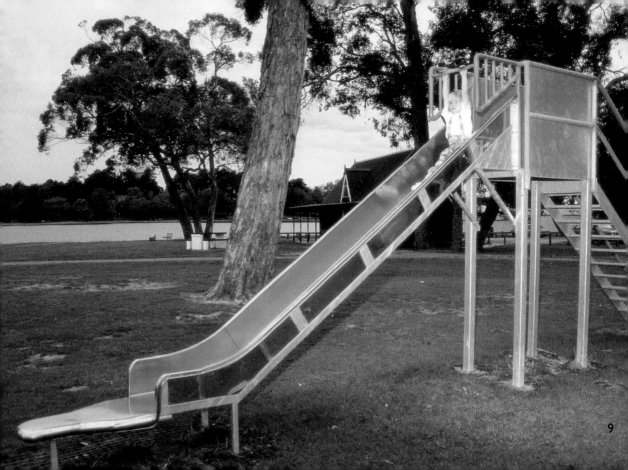

She is up

on the swing.

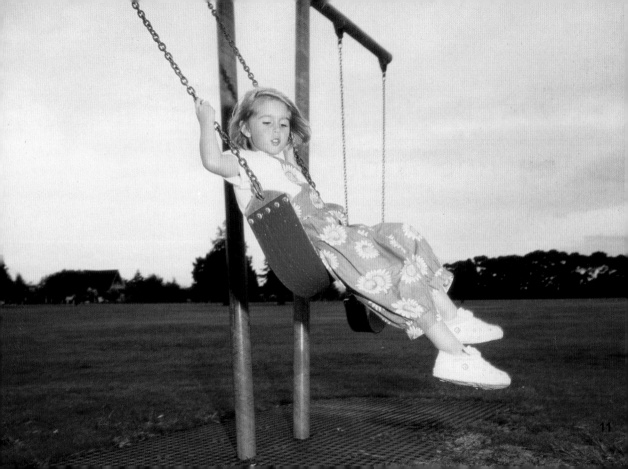

She is up
on the stool.

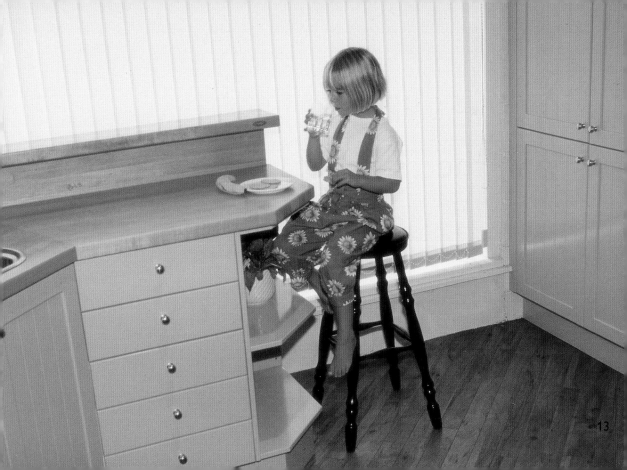

She is up
on the ladder.

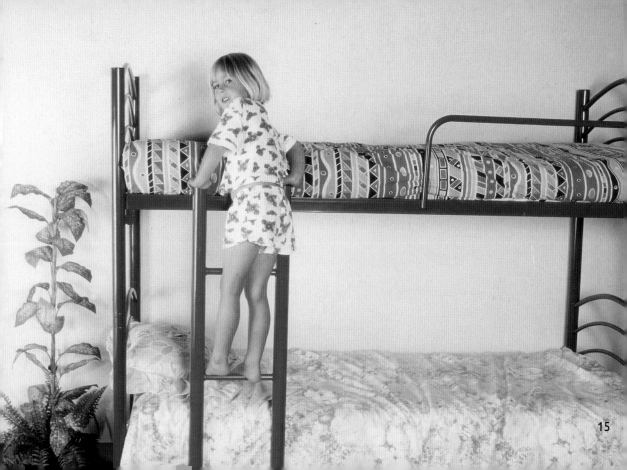

She is up
on the bunk.

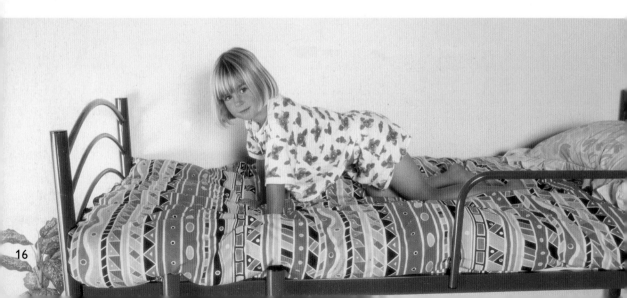